THE EQUINE LISTENOLOGY 2022 DIARY

by Elaine Heney

THE LISTENOLOGY DIARY

Copyright © 2021 by Elaine Heney

All rights reserved. No part of this publication may be reproduced, distributed, or transmitted in any form or by any means, including photocopying, recording, or other electronic or mechanical methods, without the prior written permission of the publisher.

First Edition Oct 2021

Illustrations by Faye Hobson
Published by Grey Pony Films
www.greyponyfilms.com

Meet Elaine, Ozzie & Matilda

Elaine Heney is an Irish horsewoman, film producer at Grey Pony Films, #1 best-selling author, and director of the award-winning 'Listening to the Horse™' documentary. She has helped over 120,000+ horse owners in 113 countries to create wonderful relationships with their horses. Elaine's mission is to make the world a better place for the horse. She lives in Ireland with her horses Ozzie & Matilda.

Join our facebook community:
www.starthorselistening.com

Fancy a movie night?

Listening to the Horse is the docu-series created by Elaine Heney. This 7 part award-winning documentary features over 70+ of the world's most inspiring horse people including Mark Rashid, Jim Masterson, Dr. Robert Miller, Jeff Sanders, Steve Halfpenny, Eitan Beth-Halachmy, Lester Buckley, Smokie Brannaman, Elaine Heney, Carolyn Resnick, Warwick Schiller, Guy McLean, Kim Walnes, Dagmar, Julie Goodnight, Karen Rohlf and many more.

Watch episode 1 today.

Get your free movie ticket:
www.listentothehorse.com

Online horse training courses

Elaine Heney has created a series of much loved online **groundwork & riding courses.** Visit Grey Pony Films & get started today.

www.greyponyfilms.com

Other Books In This Series

The Equine Listenology Guide
The Equine Listenology Workbook
The Equine Listenology Journal
The Equine Listenology Notebook

"Break one large goal down into lots of smaller goals, to increase your chances of success. And remember to be patient." Elaine Heney.

2022
Calendar

JANUARY

m	t	w	t	f	s	s
					01	02
03	04	05	06	07	08	09
10	11	12	13	14	15	16
17	18	19	20	21	22	23
24	25	26	27	28	29	30
31						

FEBRUARY

m	t	w	t	f	s	s
	01	02	03	04	05	06
07	08	09	10	11	12	13
14	15	16	17	18	19	20
21	22	23	24	25	26	27
28						

MARCH

m	t	w	t	f	s	s
	01	02	03	04	05	06
07	08	09	10	11	12	13
14	15	16	17	18	19	20
21	22	23	24	25	26	27
28	29	30	31			

APRIL

m	t	w	t	f	s	s
				01	02	03
04	05	06	07	08	09	10
11	12	13	14	15	16	17
18	19	20	21	22	23	24
25	26	27	28	29	30	

MAY

m	t	w	t	f	s	s
						01
02	03	04	05	06	07	08
09	10	11	12	13	14	15
16	17	18	19	20	21	22
23	24	25	26	27	28	29
30	31					

JUNE

m	t	w	t	f	s	s
		01	02	03	04	05
06	07	08	09	10	11	12
13	14	15	16	17	18	19
20	21	22	23	24	25	26
27	28	29	30			

JULY

m	t	w	t	f	s	s
				01	02	03
04	05	06	07	08	09	10
11	12	13	14	15	16	17
18	19	20	21	22	23	24
25	26	27	28	29	30	31

AUGUST

m	t	w	t	f	s	s
01	02	03	04	05	06	07
08	09	10	11	12	13	14
15	16	17	18	19	20	21
22	23	24	25	26	27	28
29	30	31				

SEPTEMBER

m	t	w	t	f	s	s
			01	02	03	04
05	06	07	08	09	10	11
12	13	14	15	16	17	18
19	20	21	22	23	24	25
26	27	28	29	30		

OCTOBER

m	t	w	t	f	s	s
					01	02
03	04	05	06	07	08	09
10	11	12	13	14	15	16
17	18	19	20	21	22	23
24	25	26	27	28	29	30
31						

NOVEMBER

m	t	w	t	f	s	s
	01	02	03	04	05	06
07	08	09	10	11	12	13
14	15	16	17	18	19	20
21	22	23	24	25	26	27
28	29	30				

DECEMBER

m	t	w	t	f	s	s
			01	02	03	04
05	06	07	08	09	10	11
12	13	14	15	16	17	18
19	20	21	22	23	24	25
26	27	28	29	30	31	

JAN/01

M	T	W	T	F	S	S
					01	02
03	04	05	06	07	08	09
10	11	12	13	14	15	16
17	18	19	20	21	22	23
24	25	26	27	28	29	30
31						

FEB/02

M	T	W	T	F	S	S
	01	02	03	04	05	06
07	08	09	10	11	12	13
14	15	16	17	18	19	20
21	22	23	24	25	26	27
28						

MAR/03

M	T	W	T	F	S	S
	01	02	03	04	05	06
07	08	09	10	11	12	13
14	15	16	17	18	19	20
21	22	23	24	25	26	27
28	29	30	31			

APR/04

M	T	W	T	F	S	S
				01	02	03
04	05	06	07	08	09	10
11	12	13	14	15	16	17
18	19	20	21	22	23	24
25	26	27	28	29	30	

MAY/05

M	T	W	T	F	S	S
						01
02	03	04	05	06	07	08
09	10	11	12	13	14	15
16	17	18	19	20	21	22
23	24	25	26	27	28	29
30	31					

JUN/06

M	T	W	T	F	S	S
		01	02	03	04	05
06	07	08	09	10	11	12
13	14	15	16	17	18	19
20	21	22	23	24	25	26
27	28	29	30			

JUL/07

M	T	W	T	F	S	S
				01	02	03
04	05	06	07	08	09	10
11	12	13	14	15	16	17
18	19	20	21	22	23	24
25	26	27	28	29	30	31

AUG/08

M	T	W	T	F	S	S
01	02	03	04	05	06	07
08	09	10	11	12	13	14
15	16	17	18	19	20	21
22	23	24	25	26	27	28
29	30	31				

SEP/09

M	T	W	T	F	S	S
			01	02	03	04
05	06	07	08	09	10	11
12	13	14	15	16	17	18
19	20	21	22	23	24	25
26	27	28	29	30		

OCT/10

M	T	W	T	F	S	S
					01	02
03	04	05	06	07	08	09
10	11	12	13	14	15	16
17	18	19	20	21	22	23
24	25	26	27	28	29	30
31						

NOV/11

M	T	W	T	F	S	S
	01	02	03	04	05	06
07	08	09	10	11	12	13
14	15	16	17	18	19	20
21	22	23	24	25	26	27
28	29	30				

DEC/12

M	T	W	T	F	S	S
			01	02	03	04
05	06	07	08	09	10	11
12	13	14	15	16	17	18
19	20	21	22	23	24	25
26	27	28	29	30	31	

January 2022

"Life is a daring adventure with horses"

monthly PLANNER

Goals

Goal #1
Get Pippin hacking out happily at a walk

Goal #2
Teach Pippin to stand still while mounting & teach backing up

Goal #3
Get outside leg behind the girth to make sure cantering on the right lead.

Remeber
Right rein is my weak leg... work on getting it to move back

#1 Thing to Improve

- Check diagonals (trot)
- Canter Transition

Reflection
If I am on the right rein my right sholder is pointing to the middle of the school.

MONTHLY TO DO LIST

- [ ] ....
- [ ] ....
- [ ] ....
- [ ] ....
- [ ] ....
- [ ] ....
- [ ] ....
- [ ] ....
- [ ] ....
- [ ] ....
- [ ] ....
- [ ] ....
- [ ] ....
- [ ] ....
- [ ] ....
- [ ] ....
- [ ] ....
- [ ] ....
- [ ] ....
- [ ] ....

MONTHLY TO DO LIST

- [ ]
- [ ]
- [ ]
- [ ]
- [ ]
- [ ]
- [ ]
- [ ]
- [ ]
- [ ]
- [ ]
- [ ]
- [ ]
- [ ]
- [ ]
- [ ]
- [ ]
- [ ]
- [ ]
- [ ]

JAN 01 TO 02

SAT

SUN

NOTES

JAN 03 TO 09

MON

TUE

WED

THU

FRI

SAT

SUN

NOTES

JAN 10 TO 16

MON

TUE

WED

THU

FRI

SAT

SUN

NOTES

JAN 17 TO 23

MON

TUE

WED

THU

FRI

SAT

SUN

NOTES

JAN 24 TO 30

MON

TUE

WED

THU

FRI
1st lesson with Northern Lights Riding Club on Nellie.

SAT
Take Rosie & Pippin out to Fiona's.
Reenie on Rosie
Getting Pippin used to other horses.

SUN

NOTES

JAN 31 TO FEB 06

MON

TUE

WED

THU

FRI

SAT

SUN

NOTES

'AHA' MOMENTS TO REMEMBER

NOTES

NOTES

NOTES

NOTES

NOTES

Doodles & Drawings

FEBRUARY 2022

*"Work with the horse in their time,
using the speed of trust."*

monthly PLANNER

Goals

Goal #1
Get saddle for Pippin

Goal #2
Ride Rosie more

Goal #3

Remeber

#1 Thing to Improve

canter transitions

Reflection

MONTHLY TO DO LIST

- [ ] Ring Bellisle
- [ ]
- [ ]
- [ ]
- [ ]
- [ ]
- [ ]
- [ ]
- [ ]
- [ ]
- [ ]
- [ ]
- [ ]
- [ ]
- [ ]
- [ ]
- [ ]
- [ ]
- [ ] Ring Bellisle
- [ ]
- [ ]

MONTHLY TO DO LIST

- [ ]
- [ ]
- [ ]
- [ ]
- [ ]
- [ ]
- [ ]
- [ ]
- [ ]
- [ ]
- [ ]
- [ ]
- [ ]
- [ ]
- [ ]
- [ ]
- [ ]
- [ ]
- [ ]
- [ ]

MONTHLY TO DO LIST

- [ ]
- [ ]
- [ ]
- [ ]
- [ ]
- [ ]
- [ ]
- [ ]
- [ ]
- [ ]
- [ ]
- [ ]
- [ ]
- [ ]
- [ ]
- [ ]
- [ ]
- [ ]
- [ ]
- [ ]

FEB 07 TO 13

MON

TUE

WED

THU

FRI

10 weeks

SAT

SUN

Show Jumping   Eglington

NOTES

FEB 14 TO 20

MON

TUE

WED

THU

FRI
Riding Lesson   NLRC
90th Dinner Dance   Young Farmers

9 weeks

SAT

SUN

NOTES

FEB 21 TO 27

MON

TUE

WED Music Society Formal

THU

FRI

Church concert with Erin

8 weeks

SAT

SUN

NOTES

FEB 28 TO MAR 06

MON

TUE

WED

THU

FRI
Waitress   Belfast with Abigail

7 weeks

SAT
Dog + House Sitting   Luke + Michelle

SUN
Dressage ?
Knockagh view Equestrian centre

Dog + House sitting   Luke + Michelle

NOTES

'AHA' MOMENTS TO REMEMBER

NOTES

NOTES

NOTES

NOTES

NOTES

Doodles & Drawings

MARCH 2022

"Whispering to a horse is about as useful as a chocolate teapot. But when you're listening to the horse, you can change their world."

monthly
PLANNER

Goals

Goal #1

_____
_____
_____

Goal #2

_____
_____
_____

Goal #3

_____
_____
_____

Reflection

Remeber

#1 Thing to Improve

_____
_____
_____

MONTHLY TO DO LIST

- [ ] ....
- [ ] ....
- [ ] ....
- [ ] ....
- [ ] ....
- [ ] ....
- [ ] ....
- [ ] ....
- [ ] ....
- [ ] ....
- [ ] ....
- [ ] ....
- [ ] ....
- [ ] ....
- [ ] ....
- [ ] ....
- [ ] ....
- [ ] ....
- [ ] ....
- [ ] ....

MAR 07 TO 13

MON: Dog + House Sitting Luke + Michelle

TUE:

WED:

THU:

FRI

6 weeks

SAT

Music @ teaparty   Macosquin w/ Erin

SUN

NOTES

MAR 14 TO 20

MON

TUE

WED

THU

FRI

5 weeks

SAT

NLRC Hack in Aghadowey   £5

SUN

NOTES

MAR 21 TO 27

MON

TUE

WED

THU

FRI

4 weeks

SAT

SUN

NOTES

MAR 28 TO APR 3

MON

TUE

WED

THU
Chancellor Choir Concert

FRI

3 weeks
NLRC Lesson 8pm

SAT

SUN

Dublin

NOTES

'AHA' MOMENTS TO REMEMBER

NOTES

NOTES

NOTES

NOTES

NOTES

Doodles & Drawings

APRIL 2022

Join our Facebook community at:

www.starthorselistening.com

monthly PLANNER

Goals

Goal #1
_____
_____
_____

Goal #2
_____
_____
_____

Goal #3
_____
_____
_____

Remeber

#1 Thing to Improve
_____
_____
_____

Reflection

MONTHLY TO DO LIST

- [ ] ....
- [ ] ....
- [ ] ....
- [ ] ....
- [ ] ....
- [ ] ....
- [ ] ....
- [ ] ....
- [ ] ....
- [ ] ....
- [ ] ....
- [ ] ....
- [ ] ....
- [ ] ....
- [ ] ....
- [ ] ....
- [ ] ....
- [ ] ....
- [ ] ....
- [ ] ....

MONTHLY TO DO LIST

- [ ] ....
- [ ] ....
- [ ] ....
- [ ] ....
- [ ] ....
- [ ] ....
- [ ] ....
- [ ] ....
- [ ] ....
- [ ] ....
- [ ] ....
- [ ] ....
- [ ] ....
- [ ] ....
- [ ] ....
- [ ] ....
- [ ] ....
- [ ] ....
- [ ] ....
- [ ] ....

MONTHLY TO DO LIST

- [ ] ....
- [ ] ....
- [ ] ....
- [ ] ....
- [ ] ....
- [ ] ....
- [ ] ....
- [ ] ....
- [ ] ....
- [ ] ....
- [ ] ....
- [ ] ....
- [ ] ....
- [ ] ....
- [ ] ....
- [ ] ....
- [ ] ....
- [ ] ....
- [ ] ....
- [ ] ....

APR 04 TO 10

MON — Dublin

TUE — Dublin

WED

THU

FRI

2 weeks

SAT

SUN

NOTES

APR 11 TO 17

MON

TUE

WED

THU

FRI
1 week to go!

SAT
NLRC Dirraw

SUN

NOTES

APR 18 TO 24

MON

TUE

WED

THU

FRI
Lu lu Due !!
NLRC Lessons

SAT

SUN

NOTES

APR 25 TO MAY 01

MON

TUE

WED

THU

FRI

SAT

SUN
Interteam Showjumping   knockaghview

NOTES

'AHA' MOMENTS TO REMEMBER

NOTES

NOTES

NOTES

NOTES

NOTES

Doodles & Drawings

May 2022

Get a free movie ticket at:

www.listentothehorse.com

monthly PLANNER

Goals

Goal #1
_____
_____
_____

Goal #2
_____
_____
_____

Goal #3
_____
_____
_____

Remeber

#1 Thing to Improve
_____
_____
_____
_____

Reflection

MONTHLY TO DO LIST

- [ ] ....
- [ ] ....
- [ ] ....
- [ ] ....
- [ ] ....
- [ ] ....
- [ ] ....
- [ ] ....
- [ ] ....
- [ ] ....
- [ ] ....
- [ ] ....
- [ ] ....
- [ ] ....
- [ ] ....
- [ ] ....
- [ ] ....
- [ ] ....
- [ ] ....
- [ ] ....

MONTHLY TO DO LIST

- [ ]
- [ ]
- [ ]
- [ ]
- [ ]
- [ ]
- [ ]
- [ ]
- [ ]
- [ ]
- [ ]
- [ ]
- [ ]
- [ ]
- [ ]
- [ ]
- [ ]
- [ ]
- [ ]
- [ ]
- [ ]
- [ ]

MONTHLY TO DO LIST

- [ ] ....
- [ ] ....
- [ ] ....
- [ ] ....
- [ ] ....
- [ ] ....
- [ ] ....
- [ ] ....
- [ ] ....
- [ ] ....
- [ ] ....
- [ ] ....
- [ ] ....
- [ ] ....
- [ ] ....
- [ ] ....
- [ ] ....
- [ ] ....
- [ ] ....
- [ ] ....

MAY 02 TO MAY 08

MON: Rebecca & Philip Henry Wedding

TUE:

WED:

THU:

FRI

SAT

SUN

NOTES

MAY 9 TO MAY 15

MON

TUE

WED

THU

FRI

SAT

SUN
Showjumping   Eglington   NLRC

NOTES

MAY 16 TO MAY 22

MON

TUE

WED

THU

FRI

SAT

SUN

NOTES

MAY 23 TO MAY 29

MON

TUE

WED

THU

FRI

SAT

SUN

NOTES

MAY 30 TO JUNE 5

MON

TUE

WED

THU

FRI

SAT

SUN

NOTES

'AHA' MOMENTS TO REMEMBER

NOTES

NOTES

NOTES

NOTES

NOTES

Doodles & Drawings

June 2022

Join our Facebook community at:

www.starthorselistening.com

monthly PLANNER

Goals

Goal #1
___
___
___

Goal #2
___
___
___

Goal #3
___
___
___

Remeber

#1 Thing to Improve
___
___
___

Reflection

MONTHLY TO DO LIST

- [ ] ....
- [ ] ....
- [ ] ....
- [ ] ....
- [ ] ....
- [ ] ....
- [ ] ....
- [ ] ....
- [ ] ....
- [ ] ....
- [ ] ....
- [ ] ....
- [ ] ....
- [ ] ....
- [ ] ....
- [ ] ....
- [ ] ....
- [ ] ....
- [ ] ....
- [ ] ....

JUNE 6 TO 12

MON

TUE

WED

THU

FRI

SAT

SUN

NOTES

JUNE 13 TO 19

MON

TUE

WED

THU

FRI

SAT

SUN

NOTES

JUNE 20 TO 26

MON

TUE

WED

THU

FRI

SAT

SUN

NOTES

NUNE 27 TO JULY 3

MON

TUE

WED

THU

FRI

SAT

SUN

NOTES

'AHA' MOMENTS TO REMEMBER

NOTES

NOTES

NOTES

NOTES

NOTES

Doodles & Drawings

July 2022

Get a free bitless bridle guide at:

www.bitlessbridleguide.com

monthly PLANNER

Goals

Goal #1
_____
_____
_____

Goal #2
_____
_____
_____

Goal #3
_____
_____
_____

Remeber

#1 Thing to Improve
_____
_____
_____

Reflection

MONTHLY TO DO LIST

- [ ]
- [ ]
- [ ]
- [ ]
- [ ]
- [ ]
- [ ]
- [ ]
- [ ]
- [ ]
- [ ]
- [ ]
- [ ]
- [ ]
- [ ]
- [ ]
- [ ]
- [ ]
- [ ]
- [ ]
- [ ]
- [ ]

MONTHLY TO DO LIST

- [ ] ....
- [ ] ....
- [ ] ....
- [ ] ....
- [ ] ....
- [ ] ....
- [ ] ....
- [ ] ....
- [ ] ....
- [ ] ....
- [ ] ....
- [ ] ....
- [ ] ....
- [ ] ....
- [ ] ....
- [ ] ....
- [ ] ....
- [ ] ....
- [ ] ....
- [ ] ....

MONTHLY TO DO LIST

- [ ]
- [ ]
- [ ]
- [ ]
- [ ]
- [ ]
- [ ]
- [ ]
- [ ]
- [ ]
- [ ]
- [ ]
- [ ]
- [ ]
- [ ]
- [ ]
- [ ]
- [ ]
- [ ]
- [ ]

JUL 04 TO 10

MON

TUE

WED

THU

FRI

SAT

SUN

NOTES

JULY 11 TO 17

MON

TUE

WED

THU

FRI

SAT

SUN

NOTES

JULY 18 TO 24

MON

TUE

WED

THU

FRI

SAT

SUN

NOTES

JULY 25 TO 31

MON

TUE

WED

THU

FRI

SAT

SUN

NOTES

'AHA' MOMENTS TO REMEMBER

NOTES

NOTES

NOTES

NOTES

NOTES

Doodles & Drawings

AUGUST 2022

Enjoy some fun polework exercises at:

www.poleworkexercises.com

monthly PLANNER

Goals

Goal #1
_____
_____
_____

Goal #2
_____
_____
_____

Goal #3
_____
_____
_____

Remeber

#1 Thing to Improve

_____
_____
_____

Reflection

MONTHLY TO DO LIST

- [ ]
- [ ]
- [ ]
- [ ]
- [ ]
- [ ]
- [ ]
- [ ]
- [ ]
- [ ]
- [ ]
- [ ]
- [ ]
- [ ]
- [ ]
- [ ]
- [ ]
- [ ]
- [ ]
- [ ]
- [ ]

AUG 01 TO 07

MON

TUE

WED

THU

FRI

SAT

SUN

NOTES

AUG 08 TO 14

MON

TUE

WED

THU

FRI

SAT

SUN

NOTES

AUG 15 TO 21

MON

TUE

WED

THU

FRI

SAT

Alison 'McDowell' Wedding

SUN

NOTES

AUG 22 TO 28

MON

TUE

WED

THU

FRI

SAT

SUN

NOTES

AUG 29 TO SEPT 04

MON

TUE

WED

THU

FRI

SAT

SUN

NOTES

'AHA' MOMENTS TO REMEMBER

NOTES

NOTES

NOTES

NOTES

NOTES

Doodles & Drawings

SEPT 2022

Enjoy some fun liberty exercises at:

www.dancingatliberty.com

monthly
PLANNER

Goals

Goal #1
___
___
___

Goal #2
___
___
___

Goal #3
___
___
___

Remeber

#1 Thing to Improve
___
___
___

Reflection

MONTHLY TO DO LIST

- [ ]
- [ ]
- [ ]
- [ ]
- [ ]
- [ ]
- [ ]
- [ ]
- [ ]
- [ ]
- [ ]
- [ ]
- [ ]
- [ ]
- [ ]
- [ ]
- [ ]
- [ ]
- [ ]
- [ ]
- [ ]
- [ ]

MONTHLY TO DO LIST

- [ ] ....
- [ ] ....
- [ ] ....
- [ ] ....
- [ ] ....
- [ ] ....
- [ ] ....
- [ ] ....
- [ ] ....
- [ ] ....
- [ ] ....
- [ ] ....
- [ ] ....
- [ ] ....
- [ ] ....
- [ ] ....
- [ ] ....
- [ ] ....
- [ ] ....
- [ ] ....

MONTHLY TO DO LIST

- [ ]
- [ ]
- [ ]
- [ ]
- [ ]
- [ ]
- [ ]
- [ ]
- [ ]
- [ ]
- [ ]
- [ ]
- [ ]
- [ ]
- [ ]
- [ ]
- [ ]
- [ ]
- [ ]
- [ ]

SEPT 05 TO 11

MON

TUE

WED

THU

FRI

SAT

SUN

NOTES

SEPT 12 TO 18

MON

TUE

WED

THU

FRI

SAT

SUN

NOTES

SEPT 19 TO 25

MON

TUE

WED

THU

FRI

SAT

SUN

NOTES

SEPT 26 TO OCT 02

MON

TUE

WED

THU

FRI

SAT

SUN

NOTES

'AHA' MOMENTS TO REMEMBER

NOTES

NOTES

NOTES

NOTES

NOTES

Doodles & Drawings

OCT 2022

"Some people think I'm weird to do groundwork. I think they are weird not to."

monthly
PLANNER

Goals

Goal #1

_____
_____
_____

Goal #2

_____
_____
_____

Goal #3

_____
_____
_____

Remeber

#1 Thing to Improve

_____
_____
_____

Reflection

MONTHLY TO DO LIST

- [ ]
- [ ]
- [ ]
- [ ]
- [ ]
- [ ]
- [ ]
- [ ]
- [ ]
- [ ]
- [ ]
- [ ]
- [ ]
- [ ]
- [ ]
- [ ]
- [ ]
- [ ]
- [ ]
- [ ]

MONTHLY TO DO LIST

- [ ] ....
- [ ] ....
- [ ] ....
- [ ] ....
- [ ] ....
- [ ] ....
- [ ] ....
- [ ] ....
- [ ] ....
- [ ] ....
- [ ] ....
- [ ] ....
- [ ] ....
- [ ] ....
- [ ] ....
- [ ] ....
- [ ] ....
- [ ] ....
- [ ] ....
- [ ] ....

MONTHLY TO DO LIST

- [ ] ....
- [ ] ....
- [ ] ....
- [ ] ....
- [ ] ....
- [ ] ....
- [ ] ....
- [ ] ....
- [ ] ....
- [ ] ....
- [ ] ....
- [ ] ....
- [ ] ....
- [ ] ....
- [ ] ....
- [ ] ....
- [ ] ....
- [ ] ....
- [ ] ....
- [ ] ....

OCT 03 TO 09

MON

TUE

WED

THU

FRI

SAT

SUN

NOTES

OCT 10 TO 16

MON

TUE

WED

THU

FRI

SAT

SUN

NOTES

OCT 17 TO 23

MON

TUE

WED

THU

FRI

SAT

SUN

NOTES

OCT 24 TO 30

MON

TUE

WED

THU

FRI

SAT

SUN

NOTES

OCT 31 TO NOV 06

MON

TUE

WED

THU

FRI

SAT

SUN

NOTES

'AHA' MOMENTS TO REMEMBER

NOTES

NOTES

NOTES

NOTES

NOTES

Doodles & Drawings

NOV 2022

"I understand that my greatest judge is my horse. So I work to put my horse's physical and mental health first, regardless of what anyone else might say."

monthly
PLANNER

Goals

Goal #1

_____
_____
_____

Goal #2

_____
_____
_____

Goal #3

_____
_____
_____

Remeber

#1 Thing to Improve

_____
_____
_____

Reflection

MONTHLY TO DO LIST

- [ ]
- [ ]
- [ ]
- [ ]
- [ ]
- [ ]
- [ ]
- [ ]
- [ ]
- [ ]
- [ ]
- [ ]
- [ ]
- [ ]
- [ ]
- [ ]
- [ ]
- [ ]
- [ ]
- [ ]

NOV 07 TO 13

MON

TUE

WED

THU

FRI

SAT

SUN

NOTES

NOV 14 TO 20

MON

TUE

WED

THU

FRI

SAT

SUN

NOTES

NOV 21 TO 27

MON

TUE

WED

THU

FRI

SAT

SUN

NOTES

NOV 28 TO DEC 04

MON

TUE

WED

THU

FRI

SAT

SUN

NOTES

'AHA' MOMENTS TO REMEMBER

NOTES

NOTES

NOTES

NOTES

NOTES

Doodles & Drawings

DEC 2022

"If you teach your horse something while there is worry in his eyes, there are two chances he'll remember. Not likely, and zero."

monthly PLANNER

Goals

Goal #1
_____
_____
_____

Goal #2
_____
_____
_____

Goal #3
_____
_____
_____

Remeber

#1 Thing to Improve
_____
_____
_____

Reflection

MONTHLY TO DO LIST

- [ ]
- [ ]
- [ ]
- [ ]
- [ ]
- [ ]
- [ ]
- [ ]
- [ ]
- [ ]
- [ ]
- [ ]
- [ ]
- [ ]
- [ ]
- [ ]
- [ ]
- [ ]
- [ ]
- [ ]

MONTHLY TO DO LIST

MONTHLY TO DO LIST

- [ ] ....
- [ ] ....
- [ ] ....
- [ ] ....
- [ ] ....
- [ ] ....
- [ ] ....
- [ ] ....
- [ ] ....
- [ ] ....
- [ ] ....
- [ ] ....
- [ ] ....
- [ ] ....
- [ ] ....
- [ ] ....
- [ ] ....
- [ ] ....
- [ ] ....
- [ ] ....

DEC 05 TO 11

MON

TUE

WED

THU

FRI

SAT

SUN

NOTES

DEC 12 TO 18

MON

TUE

WED

THU

FRI

SAT

SUN

NOTES

DEC 19 TO 25

MON

TUE

WED

THU

FRI

SAT

SUN

NOTES

DEC 26 TO JAN 1

MON

TUE

WED

THU

FRI

SAT

SUN

NOTES

'AHA' MOMENTS TO REMEMBER

NOTES

NOTES

NOTES

NOTES

NOTES

Doodles & Drawings

2022

YOUR YEAR IN REVIEW

2022 ACCOMPLISHMENTS

2022 ACCOMPLISHMENTS

2022 ACCOMPLISHMENTS

2022 ACCOMPLISHMENTS

2022 ACCOMPLISHMENTS

2022 ACCOMPLISHMENTS

2022 ACCOMPLISHMENTS

2022 ACCOMPLISHMENTS

2022 'AHA' MOMENTS TO REMEMBER

2022 'AHA' MOMENTS TO REMEMBER

2022 'AHA' MOMENTS TO REMEMBER

2022 'AHA' MOMENTS TO REMEMBER

2022 'AHA' MOMENTS TO REMEMBER

2022 'AHA' MOMENTS TO REMEMBER

2022 PHOTO MEMORIES

2022 PHOTO MEMORIES

2022 PHOTO MEMORIES

2022 PHOTO MEMORIES

2022 PHOTO MEMORIES

2022 PHOTO MEMORIES

2022 PHOTO MEMORIES

2022 NOTES

2022 NOTES

2022 NOTES

2022 NOTES

2022 NOTES

2022 NOTES

2022 NOTES

2022 NOTES

ONLINE HORSE TRAINING COURSES

Elaine Heney has created a much loved series of online polework, liberty, lateral, groundwork & riding programs. Visit Grey Pony Films online & learn more:

www.greyponyfilms.com

Printed in Great Britain
by Amazon